JOAN of ARC

"Having been lost through a woman,
[the kingdom of France] would be
restored by a girl from Lorraine."

—Old French prophecy

Landmarks in History

JOAN of ARC

by Nancy Wilson Ross

Random House 🏛 New York

www.randomhouse.com/kids

Library of Congress Cataloging-in-Publication Data
Ross, Nancy Wilson, 1901–1986.
Joan of Arc / by Nancy Wilson Ross. p. cm. – (Landmark books)
SUMMARY: A biography of the fifteenth-century peasant girl who led a
French army to victory against the English, witnessed the crowning of
King Charles VII, and was later burned at the stake for witchcraft.
[1. Joan, of Arc, Saint, 1412–1431–Juvenile literature.
2. Christian women saints–France–Biography–Juvenile literature.
3. Hundred Years' War, 1339–1453–Juvenile literature.
4. France–History–Charles VII, 1422–1461–Juvenile literature.
[1. Joan, of Arc, Saint, 1412–1431. 2. Saints. 3. Women–Biography.
4. France–History–Charles VII, 1422–1461.] I. Title.
dc103.5.R67 1999 944'.026'092–dc21 [B] 98-51932
ISBN: 0-375-80232-0 (trade) ISBN: 0-375-90232-5 (lib. bdg.)

Printed in the United States of America
10 9 8 7 6 5 4 3 2 1

LANDMARK BOOKS, RANDOM HOUSE, and colophons are
registered trademarks of Random House, Inc.

This book is most respectfully dedicated to:

My three stepchildren:
Aline, Cecily, and *Christopher.*

My three nephews:
Charles, Jr., Robert, and *Michael.*

My one niece:
Catherine.

My four godchildren:
Cathy M., Willard, Stuart III, and *T. E., Jr.*

And an assorted group of young friends
including—alphabetically:

Amanda and *Ann*
and *Brooksie.*
Camilla and *Carey,*
Chama and *Cheli,*
Clyde and *Danna,*
David and *Eddie*
and *Gary.*
Jane and *Jeremy,*
Kate and *Kathryn,*
Lee and *Linda* and *Lucy.*
Marianne and *Michael S.,*
Peter, Jr., and *Pierre,*
Roger III and *Searle.*
Stephen B., and *Stephen S.,*
Susan H., and *Susan K.,*
Timmy, Toby, and *Victoria.*

CONTENTS

1

The Savior of France Is Born

Near the end of one of the longest wars in history, the war between France and England known as the Hundred Years' War, a little girl was born to some simple farming people named d'Arc. Their home was in the village of Domrémy, in the eastern part of France.

The day of her birth was twelve days after Christmas. The year was 1412.

If you had been one of the neighbors who came to the humble farmhouse to greet the new little d'Arc baby in her plain wooden cradle, you would have probably thought her a very ordinary child.

When she was christened and given the name of Joan (Jeanne, as they spell it in France) she cried in protest just as all babies do when unexpectedly splashed with water. No one among the onlookers at this historic moment guessed how great this child's future was to be. Certainly her parents never imagined that their little black-eyed, black-haired baby was destined to be one of the most remarkable girls in all history, Joan of Arc, the Savior of France.

Joan's family name was d'Arc, but the French word *de*—sometimes shortened simply to *d'*—means "of" in English, and so Jeanne d'Arc became in English "Joan of Arc." Her own countrymen, during her lifetime, often called her simply "the Maid."

The Maid's strange and wonderful career began when she was just thirteen years old. By seventeen she was already winning battles in which trained military men had failed. Her adventures and experiences are so fascinating that hundreds of books have been written about her.

People are still trying to explain how this simple farm girl was able to inspire deeds of superhuman bravery among her soldiers, plan military campaigns with the wisdom of a general, and get a Prince crowned as King of France.

In the fifteenth century, when Joan lived, her enemies finally decided she was a witch. Much later—five hundred years later—the Roman Catholic Church decided that she was a saint. People who do not consider her either still have to admit that she was an extraordinary person.

2

How We Know So Much About Joan of Arc

We know much more about Joan of Arc than is usually known about famous people who lived in the distant past. We owe this to the records that were kept at her various trials for witchcraft.

The documents that have been handed down to us tell in great detail how Joan spent her whole life. We know, from her relatives and neighbors, about her daily existence from childhood on. We know what she ate and drank, what she wore, whom she knew, what she said and did.

These court recordings manage to tell us almost everything we want to know about Joan—except one thing. They have never explained the central mystery of her life. This mystery was the guidance of the strange "Voices" who Joan claimed had told her, from the age of thirteen, what her destiny was to be.

3

Joan First Hears Her Voices

Joan was just thirteen years of age when she first heard the Voices that told her she was to be the Savior of France.

She was standing in her father's garden in the village of Domrémy. It was at noontime. Suddenly she heard a mysterious, beautiful Voice speaking to her. At the same time she seemed to see a light that was brighter than the sun.

When Joan heard the Voice and saw the light, she was, at first, terrified. But the gentleness of the Voice caused all fear to leave her. The Voice urged her not to be afraid, to be a good girl, to have faith, for she was destined to accomplish miraculous things.

The Voice told her that she had been chosen to restore peace to the Kingdom of France. She was also to help protect the Crown Prince. In time she was even to see that he was crowned as King. She herself was to be present at the crowning.

When the Voice and the light disappeared, Joan must have wondered if she had imagined it all. How could she, a simple farm girl, possibly become the Savior of France? She could neither read nor write. She could not even sign her own name. Furthermore, her family was not rich or powerful. She had never been more than a mile or two from her own cottage, and never expected to go farther. How would she win the Crown of France for the poor weak Prince, called the Dauphin?

But the mysterious Voice had particularly warned her to tell no one about its message, so she obeyed.

During the four years that followed, this Voice, and other Voices, regularly visited Joan and prepared her for her mission. In all that time she told no one of these strange happenings.

How hard it must have been for a young girl to keep such a secret for so long! It would be easy to imagine her confiding in her friends, Hauviette and Mengette; perhaps even boasting a little about her unearthly visitors. For Joan was a very religious girl and she had come to believe that the Voices were sent from God.

4

Trouble in France

Joan grew up in a world full of people, old as well as young, who had never known a day of peace in all their lives. France was living through the famous Hundred Years' War.

The English and the French—along with hired soldiers called mercenaries from other parts of Europe—had been fighting on French soil as long as people could remember. '

The trouble really began when a Frenchman, William the Conqueror, went across the English Channel in the year 1066 and took over the land of England. There he set up his own dynasty.

For many years William's descendants, though now English, continued to hold sections of France.

9

Finally these English descendants of William the Conqueror decided that controlling just *part* of France was not enough for them. They wanted to control all of it. Also they wanted both countries—England and France—to be under one crown. And that crown, they insisted, must be the English one.

To make matters really complicated, not all the French people were against this plan. You might have thought that all Frenchmen would naturally want a French King. But this was not so.

France was split into warring parties. The emotion we call patriotism, or love of one's country, was just in the process of being born in Europe in the fifteenth century. Before Joan's time people tended more to think of themselves as belonging to a certain family, or village, or region. They did not think of themselves so much as being French, or English, or Italian. Joan of Arc was to be partly responsible for the birth of patriotism in her own country of France.

Although Joan lived in a remote village, a long way from such big centers as Paris or Orléans, she had heard plenty about the troubles of her country from her very childhood. She knew that there were deep divisions among her own people.

One French party sided with the Crown Prince. This Prince was the Dauphin of whom Joan's Voices had spoken.

The people who did not side with the Dauphin sided with a powerful French nobleman, known as the Duke of Burgundy. Though of French descent, the Duke was fighting on the English side.

There were many reasons for this state of affairs. Principally, the Duke of Burgundy was a very ambitious man who wanted power and didn't much care how he got it. The French people who fought on his side were called the Burgundians. They were pro-English.

When Joan spoke of her country, she often called it the "fair land of France." But this was only what she wished it to be. The French countryside was as beautiful then as it is today, but the condition of the people who lived there was far from "fair."

France was in just the kind of wretched state that any land would be on which soldiers had been quartered for seventy years.

It was not the English troops alone who raided, burned, stole, and took food from the barns and the gardens of the poor peasants. The French soldiers were just as bad. After all, they had to fight, and to fight they had to eat. But the people didn't see how the war was doing them much good, and so what the soldiers did made them very angry.

The real trouble was that the French had no aim toward which to work. They were confused and undisciplined. Worst of all, they were without hope.

The French had no hope and no discipline

because they had no leader. Their last king, Charles the Sixth, the father of the Prince called the Dauphin, had been insane. Queen Isabella, the wife of Charles the Sixth, had lived a very wicked life. When her insane husband had finally died, the Queen had opposed her own son, the Dauphin. She did not want him to inherit the French throne, as she felt she would have more power if the Burgundians won. She even went so far as to say that the Dauphin was not the King's child.

The Dauphin wanted the throne of France, but he didn't want to fight to get it. The truth is, he was a rather timid man. Everybody bullied him. No one took him very seriously. He was always in trouble about money. He had to pawn the family jewels to pay the expenses of his court. It was even said that he had to borrow money at times from his own cook. And there was gossip about the patched coat he wore because he couldn't afford a new one.

Yet for all his homely face, his weak will,

and his bad luck, he was the lawful Prince. To him belonged the right to become the King of France. So Joan's Voices had told her over and over again.

5

Joan's Voices and a Strange Dream

The days and weeks passed slowly in Domrémy. Joan took the family cows to pasture. She helped her mother spin and cook. She helped her father and brothers plant the gardens and gather the autumn harvests. She played games with her friends Hauviette and Mengette. Still, she told no one of her Voices. But she heard from them many times.

From the Voices she learned more and more about the role she was to play in the drama that was going on in other parts of France. Because she trusted her Voices, she was able to believe that she would help to foil the plots against the Prince. Because of her the wicked Queen was to fail. Because of her the Duke of Burgundy was to be defeated.

15

Because of her the English were to be driven at last from the fair land of France.

If the Royal Prince did not have the will to fight for his rights, to win his own crown and put it on his head, the little farm girl from Domrémy would do it for him. Joan had been told that she herself would be present at the crowning of the Dauphin. She would be there because she would have made the coronation possible.

Perhaps it is not so strange that she told no one about these things that were going to happen. After all, who would have believed her?

But one day when Joan was fourteen, her father, Jacques, had a dream that gave him a bad scare. He told his family he had dreamed that Joan dressed herself like a boy and went away with the armies.

Poor Jacques d'Arc was so upset by this dream that he begged his sons, Joan's brothers, to drown their sister if such a thing should ever come to pass.

16

Even when her mother told Joan about the dream her father had had, and what he had said to the boys, Joan did not confess about the Voices. They had already told her that before long she was to wear armor and lead soldiers to battle.

6

Joan Takes the First Step

It was in her sixteenth year that Joan found her first chance to start on the career for which the Voices had been preparing her.

Some cousins named Lassois who lived not far away from Domrémy were going to have a baby. Their home was in a village near the only large town of the district that remained faithful to the cause of the poor Dauphin.

Joan knew that in this town, called Vaucouleurs, there was a small army of loyal soldiers. She also knew that these soldiers were led by a bold commander named Robert de Baudricourt.

Joan determined that by some means she would get herself into the commander's presence. Once there she would demand that he give her an escort and send her to the aid of the Dauphin. So her Voices had instructed her.

The first step in this plan was not difficult. Joan's family readily gave her permission to go to help out in the Lassois household when the baby was born.

This request to go and give help was very like Joan. She frequently tended sick people among the d'Arc neighbors. She had a reputation for kindness and generosity. She had even been known to give up her bed to weary travelers passing through the village, while she herself would sleep on the hearth.

The second step in her plan was to confide in Durand Lassois, the father of the new baby.

Durand Lassois was so much older than Joan that she called him Uncle instead of Cousin. He was the first person to whom she ever described her Voices. She knew she had to confide in Uncle Durand or she would never get to see the commander of the garrison.

How was she able to convince her relative, a

19

sensible, practical peasant, that she was not crazy when she demanded that he take her to nearby Vaucouleurs to interview the famous captain Robert de Baudricourt? This very question was asked of Durand Lassois some years later. He answered by saying that Joan had been able to persuade him, in part at least, by reminding him of an old French prophecy.

According to the prophecy, the country of France, "having been lost through a woman [which was taken to refer to the wicked plots of the Dauphin's mother], would be restored by a girl from Lorraine." Joan was from the village of Domrémy, which, in turn, was in the district of Lorraine. Joan believed herself to be that girl.

Her belief was so strong that Uncle Durand could not resist it. Joan had a very powerful will when she believed she was doing what must be done. So Uncle Durand gave in and took Joan to see the commander of the garrison at Vaucouleurs.

7

Joan Meets a Tough Captain

In those days, country people frequently brought their troubles to the governors of garrison towns. Captain Robert de Baudricourt, rough, tough, and brave, was probably not very much surprised when there appeared before him a middle-aged workman and a sturdy farm girl in a patched red dress.

But he could hardly have been prepared for the request of this girl with black hair and burning dark eyes. She said she wanted immediate permission to "go into France." (Joan had been born on the extreme eastern edge of France; in fact, it is said that part of her father's farm lay in a neighboring country. For this reason she was able to speak of "going into France," though she had actually been born there.) She said she had been told to save France from the English and crown the Dauphin as King. She would need, she said gravely, a horse and a suit of armor.

After his first stare of amazement, how Robert de Baudricourt laughed! He roared and slapped his thigh with his hand. He hadn't had such a good laugh in many long, weary days. What with his own garrison in constant danger and the great city of Orléans said to be next on the English list of conquests, laughs were hard to come by.

The solemn young farm girl from Domrémy seemed not at all disturbed by the captain's laughter. She remained quiet until he stopped and began to wipe his eyes with his sleeve.

Then once more she spoke. If he would not do as she asked, would he at least send a message to the Dauphin? She said she wanted to warn the Dauphin that he must guard himself well. He must also avoid offering battle to the enemy just now, for the French were not ready at this time for offensive warfare. "Please tell him," she added, "that my Lord will send him help by spring of the coming year." The Dauphin could count on that promise, for he was "destined to be King of France."

She finished her grave little speech by saying calmly, "And by God's will I myself, with the help of my Lord, will lead him to be crowned."

The rough captain cocked one eyebrow and pursed his lips mockingly.

"And just who is this Lord of yours?" he inquired. He thought she must be referring to a feudal chief on whose domain she lived.

When Joan replied simply, "The King of Heaven," de Baudricourt again could not restrain his mirth. Once more he laughed his big roaring laugh. But only for a moment. Then he frowned.

Did she, he asked, believe that an ignorant

country girl could solve problems that the wisest men of two countries had been trying to settle for almost a hundred years?

The very idea made him angry. Didn't he have enough on his mind without being bothered by a crazy little country wench who believed herself to be a national savior?

"Off with you!" he shouted. "Get out of here! Go on home!"

He turned to her uncle Durand. "And you," he shouted fiercely, "give this girl a good boxing on her ears and then take her home and tell her father to give her a good sound spanking."

Thus ended the first visit to Vaucouleurs, the first step on Joan's mission. But she was not discouraged. She knew what she had to do. She had been told she would succeed. She would simply wait a little while and try again.

8

Home Again—and Trouble

Although we know quite a lot about Joan as a young girl, we do not know whether Uncle Durand boxed her ears as he was told. Nor do we know whether her father gave her that good sound spanking.

It seems doubtful that either of them used violence on young Joan. For one thing, in the days immediately after Joan's visit to Vaucouleurs, the people around Domrémy had plenty of other things on their minds.

English raiders descended suddenly on the countryside. Farm people like Joan's family and neighbors were forced to flee for refuge to a nearby community where there was a wall to protect them.

When they were finally able to return to

Domrémy, the d'Arcs found their cottage burned to the ground along with those of their neighbors.

Joan immediately set to work to help her family clear up the rubble, rebuild their house, and put in a late garden. As usual, she helped her mother with the cooking and the spinning, tended the family cattle, and did all her other daily chores. Meanwhile, she kept her ears open for word of the progress of distant battles. She was still certain that she would someday play a part in the wars. It took more than the laughter of the captain at Vaucouleurs to discourage Joan.

It was near Christmastime that Joan learned some very disturbing news. All over France, word had spread that the city of Orléans, described as "the center of France, the elbow of the river Loire, the key to the South," was soon to meet its great test.

This time either the English would succeed

in capturing Orléans for good and all, or their armies would be driven off. If the enemy was defeated at Orléans, France might once more look forward to better days.

This last prospect seemed hopeless, for Orléans was almost out of food. It could not carry on without supplies. And how could supplies get into a city entirely surrounded by its enemies?

When Joan heard about the plight of the city of Orléans she suddenly became wild with impatience. Her Voices had been telling her that she was not to have a very long time in which to perform her difficult tasks. Precious days were passing while she stayed on in Domrémy among the cabbages and cows. She must act soon.

On her seventeenth birthday she knew she could wait no longer. And so, shortly after the sixth day of January, in the year 1429, Joan set out on her second trip. She went straight back to Robert de Baudricourt at Vaucouleurs.

There is no record of how Joan persuaded her father to give his consent to this second trip away from home. After all, she had used the first journey to her cousin's house as an excuse for a daring adventure. But whatever went on in her parents' minds, we do know that Joan got their permission to visit the Lassois household once again.

This time when Joan rode out of Domrémy on a borrowed horse, it was for the last time. She was never to see her village or her friends again. On the back of a farm horse she was riding forth on the second step of her great destiny.

Perhaps because of the strict orders of her Voices she did not dare to say good-bye, not even to her best friend, Hauviette. History tells us that Hauviette "wept bitterly" when she learned that Joan had gone away without a farewell.

9

New Friends

When Joan came for the second time into the presence of the scornful captain, Robert de Baudricourt, he did not receive her quite so rudely as he had the first time.

For one thing, he was growing desperate about the state of affairs. His town, Vaucouleurs, was in peril. Every day he saw people deserting the seemingly hopeless cause of the Dauphin. Some of de Baudricourt's best friends were trying to persuade him to desert and cross over to the Burgundians, who were on the English side.

No wonder the captain was ready to listen to anyone—even an ignorant farm girl—who was on the Dauphin's side and who still had faith and courage!

There was something else that made de Baudricourt look on Joan with greater favor. Before she appeared for the second time, she had made a new and valuable friend who knew Robert de Baudricourt personally.

This new friend was a young nobleman named Jean de Metz. Since de Metz was to play such an important part in Joan's early career, we must tell how she met him in the first place.

While Joan was waiting for Captain de Baudricourt to give her permission to visit him for the second time, she lived with some people in Vaucouleurs named de Royer. Who the de Royers were we do not know. Perhaps they were friends of the Lassois family. At any rate, Joan lived like a daughter in their household while she impatiently waited to see the captain. As she waited, she made herself useful to Madame de Royer with spinning and other household tasks. Joan could never stay idle.

Word got around the town about the young

girl from Domrémy who was staying with the de Royers. It was said she had seen visions. In these visions she had been told she was to save France. Perhaps she was the girl of whom the old prophecy had spoken!

Jean de Metz had heard these stories about Joan. Out of curiosity and a desperate hope that it might be true, he came to the house to see the strange girl from Lorraine.

Jean de Metz was a good young man, and though of noble birth he had no false pride. When he was ushered into the little dark room where Joan sat spinning, he went straight up to her. He put out his hand and asked kindly, but bluntly, "What are you doing here anyway?"

Before Joan could reply, he demanded, "Are we all going to become English? Will the King be driven from his kingdom?"

Joan looked up at the tall, anxious young soldier and gravely replied to his questions in the order in which he put them.

"I have come here to ask Robert de Baudricourt to lead me, or to send me, with an escort to the Dauphin. He pays no attention to me. But nonetheless, before spring, I must be on my way to the Dauphin even"—and here her voice rose and became passionate with feeling—"even if I wear out my legs to the knees."

Then she added, "There is no one in all the world, neither King, nor duke, nor daughter of the King of Scotland, nor any other, who can regain the kingdom of France. There is no help for the kingdom but through me."

And then before he could speak—if indeed, he could have found a reply to such an astounding statement—she added that she would much rather be at home spinning beside her mother. Her voice broke as she said, "For these things do not belong to my station. Yet it is necessary that I go, since God wishes it."

Jean de Metz was deeply moved by this

strange girl's faith and courage. He felt that no discouragement or delay could alter her belief in what she was meant to do. He took her hand again and swore that he believed her and would help her as much as he could.

In that very first meeting she was able to infect him with her own impatient desire to act quickly, while there was still time to save France.

Jean de Metz asked her, "When shall we start?"

And she replied, without hesitation, "Better today than tomorrow, better tomorrow than any later."

10

Joan Is on Her Way at Last

Just two weeks after her first meeting with Jean de Metz, Joan, with de Baudricourt's permission, was on her way to the Dauphin.

Jean de Metz, well known as a brave soldier and a sensible man, had used his influence with the captain to persuade him to let Joan go and to give her the escort she asked for.

But still another event had helped to influence the captain to change his attitude toward Joan's mission. This was one of a number of strange events in Joan's life for which it is not easy to find an explanation.

It happened that one day, while still waiting for permission to travel to the Dauphin's court, Joan came hurrying to de Baudricourt's quarters, very troubled.

When she was admitted to his presence, she cried in a disturbed and accusing voice, "You are too slow in sending me. This very day a great disaster has befallen the gentle Dauphin, and worse events are in store for him unless you send me to his aid."

De Baudricourt laughed and told her to run along back to her spinning like a good girl. How could she know something he didn't know?

A short time afterward he received word that the French armies had been defeated a long distance away. What is stranger still, the disaster had been taking place just as Joan had entered the room to warn him. Even today we do not understand how Joan could have known this.

So at last de Baudricourt said she might go. But before she set forth he took one last precaution. He called in a priest and had him give Joan some tests to see if she was, or was not, a witch. The priest found her a "good, honest girl" and said so.

After that, de Baudricourt put no further obstacles in her way. He even came to the gates of the town to see her off on her long journey to the court of Chinon.

Joan set off with an escort of five men. These were Jean de Metz and a friend of his—a nobleman named Bertrand de Poulengy— also their two servants and a soldier called Richard the Archer. Judging from his name he must have been a specially fine marksman. He was probably taken along for added protection on the dangerous journey.

Joan had been given a horse, spurs and boots, and some hand-me-down armor. She had been outfitted by people of the town who believed in her cause and by her two new noble friends.

Jean de Metz had encouraged her to wear the clothes of a boy on the long and dangerous journey. Her Voices had also told her she was to do this. The suggestion was a very sensible one, but it was to cost her dear.

At his final parting, Robert de Baudricourt, the hardened commander, was deeply moved as he bade farewell to the strange farm girl who had first annoyed him with her persistence and finally won his respect. As the party reached the gate of the town, the captain himself put a sword in Joan's girlish hand and said, "Go—and let come what may!"

If his tone held any hint of doubts, Joan's voice did not echo it.

She replied in her usual calm manner, "The way is clear before me—for to do this deed I was born."

With a clatter of horses' hoofs on the stones of the courtyard, they made their way out of the gates of Vaucouleurs on the first lap of the long journey across France to the Dauphin.

11

Joan's Journey to the Prince

At that time, the Dauphin was living in the town of Chinon. To reach him, Joan had to ride nearly four hundred miles across France. Here, too, her determination pushed her onward, and she and her men covered between thirty and forty miles a day.

To add to their difficulties, they often had to travel at night, for the countryside was filled with bands of wandering soldiers. On these occasions, Joan's party would muffle their horses' hoofs with cloths to ensure silence as they galloped over the echoing stones.

Joan seldom dared to go by way of the bridges because of the sentries who might report her passing. If she were stopped and questioned, and it was discovered that she came from Vaucouleurs, all the members of her party might be held prisoner.

Since they could not go over the bridges, they had to swim their horses across the rivers. At other times, they might have found shallow places, or fords, where the horses could walk from one bank to the other. Unfortunately, it was near the end of February, and the thawing snow had filled the rivers with deep and swiftly moving water. Swimming a horse across a stream under such conditions and at night was not an easy task.

Throughout the journey the moon was on the wane and there was very little light. In the many forests, after nightfall, as the party picked its way among the trees, the shadows must often have looked like enemies crouched and ready to spring.

Yet in spite of all the difficulties, Joan, though not accustomed to riding horseback, kept up with her escort all the way. She even urged the men to a faster pace, so great was her impatience to get to the Dauphin and to begin the work that her Voices had commanded her to do.

At last, on the eleventh day, they saw in the distance the shining towers of the great castle of Chinon, with the little village nestled near it.

Joan had her letter to the Dauphin ready for immediate delivery. She had stopped at an inn a short distance from Chinon to dictate a message to him. Since she could not write herself, one of her traveling companions had written for her. This message announced Joan's arrival and told the Dauphin what she had come to do.

As soon as they reached Chinon, she sent off the message and then settled down to wait for a summons to court.

Joan waited three days. It was her first experience with the Dauphin's habit of putting things off. If there was a choice between doing something today or tomorrow, he always chose tomorrow.

During her three-day wait, Joan must have looked often in admiration, and even in fear, at the imposing castle of Chinon.

Joan had never seen anything to compare with this vast château that stretched its noble length along the banks of the river Vienne. Gray and massive it stood, with towers that overlooked the woods and vineyards of Touraine. Inside the castle hundreds of rooms looked out upon formal gardens. Here at Chinon the Dauphin was enjoying a luxurious life among flatterers and favorites.

The Dauphin, though a weak man, was not a bad one. He might have been expected to scoff at a message from a peasant girl who wrote to tell him she had been sent to crown him King. But he did not. One reason was because gossip about this strange girl from Domrémy had already reached his ears. He had been told that Joan claimed to be guided by mysterious Voices. Naturally he became curious, for he too had heard the old prophecy about the girl from Lorraine who was to save France.

After three days of asking everybody's advice, the Prince decided to see Joan. He sent a message summoning her to his presence.

Joan immediately obeyed, and on the way she gave another evidence of her strange powers. She had just walked up the hill across the drawbridge that led to the castle. As she was about to enter the main gate under the clock tower, a common soldier reined his horse beside her. He looked Joan up and down in her boy's clothes and spoke to her in a way that was rude and insulting.

Joan paused only long enough to reply gravely, "You do wrong to speak thus, for you are very near your death."

A number of people heard her strange words. It was less than an hour later that the soldier fell into the river and was drowned.

But no one had yet heard this remarkable story when Joan entered the great hall of the Dauphin's castle.

12

Joan Meets Her Prince at Last

A courtier in livery ushered Joan into a huge room filled with the laughter and talk of many people. The door closed behind her.

Then she was left alone. No one paid the slightest attention to the strange young girl from Lorraine.

As she waited, the light from fifty great torches shone in her dazzled eyes. It glanced off jewels and brocades, off silky furs and towering headdresses—the almost comic millinery worn by the women of those days. The clothes were unfamiliar, and so were the soft voices—unlike the rough tones of the people among whom Joan grew up.

Among all the hundreds of faces, not one looked directly at Joan. She stood all alone in the midst of the whirl of sound and color—an ignorant little farm girl with cropped black hair and the shabby garments of a boy.

But she remembered her mission. She had come to see the Dauphin. He must be in this room or the page would not have brought her here. Where, then, was he?

She looked about. No one seemed to be wearing the royal emblem that should mark a future king. Of a throne there was no sign. A great hooded fireplace occupied one end of the room. It was filled with burning logs. She looked there, too, but no regal chair of any kind could be seen near it.

For the second time a wave of fear and bewilderment rushed over her. She spoke sadly and softly. It was told later that she said, "Oh, please don't play tricks on me."

She had guessed the truth. The courtiers were trying to trick her. The Dauphin's friends had persuaded him to give no help to this unknown girl who pretended to possess such special powers. They had even persuaded him to dress less brilliantly than his courtiers so that she would find it hard to recognize him.

When, in spite of her little whispered plea, no one came to her rescue, Joan began to study the other guests quietly and deliberately. There were three hundred people in the hall. After just a few moments Joan walked straight to where the Dauphin stood with his back to her, chatting with friends. Kneeling at his feet, she made him the speech she had planned:

"Gentle Dauphin, I am Joan, the Maid. The King of Heaven sends me to you with the message that you shall be crowned in the city of Reims, and that you shall be the lieutenant of the King of Heaven, who is also the King of France."

Joan addressed the Prince as "Dauphin," although he liked to give himself the title and name of King Charles VII. It was Joan's belief, guided by her Voices, that Charles could not rightly be called King, or be accepted by the French as reigning monarch, until after his crowning at Reims. Reims was the city where, by ancient tradition, all Kings of France must be crowned.

Now, even after the girl had recognized him, the Dauphin still tried to deceive her. Attempting to lift her to her feet, he said, "You are mistaken. I am not the King."

He pointed to another, more elegantly dressed gentleman. "There is the King, over there."

But Joan only shook her head. And she would not rise from her knees. Still at his feet, looking up at him, she said, "Noble Prince, it is you and none other."

Then the Dauphin relented. He lifted her gently to her feet and led her to one side, away from the throng of people.

They spoke together privately for some time. No one knew what Joan said to him.

47

Some people believed that she convinced the Prince that his mother was speaking falsely when she said he was not the true son of the dead King Charles VI. Joan's Voices had told her that the Dauphin was the rightful heir to the throne.

Other people believed in another story. According to this, she reminded the Dauphin of a secret vow that he had made one day when praying alone in a far-distant chapel. This vow had been told to no one in the world.

Whatever it was that Joan said, everyone noticed that when the Prince returned from his conversation with the little farm girl, his face shone with new hope.

13

More New Friends and Some New Delays

Although the Dauphin had apparently accepted Joan at her first visit, the delays were not yet over. Joan's patience was to be tried by many more weeks of waiting.

The Dauphin was never able to hold one opinion or follow one course of action for any length of time. His followers soon convinced him that he must test this unknown country girl still further, for at that period in French history many strange people were claiming special powers. These unlikely powers were believed to come more often from the Devil than from Heaven. The Dauphin must make sure that the Maid from Lorraine was not really a witch.

So Joan was sent to be tested in another

town, this time by priests and professors.

During the six weeks that she was examined in the town of Poitiers, Joan answered all questions honestly, clearly, and sometimes with a show of spirit. Throughout the questions, she stuck to her stories about the Voices.

Once, one of her examiners, hoping to trip her up, asked what language was used by the Heavenly visitors—those Voices who came to her when she was alone. Joan replied naughtily, "Better French than yours." This was a slap at her rather pompous questioner, who spoke with a very crude accent.

Yes, Joan had spirit, but she was not arrogant in spite of her new standing in the world. At the very beginning of her examination she had said to her judges, "So you have come to examine me. Well, you might as well know it, I can't tell A from B."

Of course her ignorance and her inability to read or write made her unshaken belief in what she could do seem even more strange to the examining board. She outlined her program for them with her usual calm faith.

She said if they would allow her, she would first of all relieve the siege of Orléans and oust the English from that important city. As a result of this and other defeats, the English would prepare to leave France. The Dauphin would then be crowned King in Reims Cathedral. After this happy event, Paris, the beautiful, beloved city, now in the possession of the English, would be restored to France. Finally, the most famous of French dukes, the Duke of Orléans, who was a captive in England, would be returned safely to his native land.

This program took the breath of the learned gentlemen. And who can wonder? There she sat—an ignorant girl from a distant farm—wearing her scandalous boy's tunic and trousers, her equally scandalous close-cropped dark head nodding in emphasis as

51

she made the points to this solemn jury of eminent men.

Joan never stressed the miraculous side of her story. To her it was all a very simple matter. Voices came and spoke to her. She listened. She believed. She obeyed. That was all there was to it.

When the priests and professors kept pressing her to give them signs of any special powers she possessed, she finally lost her patience.

"I've not come to Poitiers to perform miracles and give signs," she cried. "Just you lead me to Orléans and I'll show you the miracles for which I have been sent."

Then she was asked a particularly difficult question: Why, if God wished to free France from its troubles, didn't He just free the country? Why were Joan and the armies needed?

To this Joan made a very intelligent reply. "People will fight the battles," she said, "and God will grant the victory."

At last the examiners gave up. Joan's stubborn faith had won. They handed down the important decision that they found nothing in her character but "honesty, simplicity, humility, maidenhood, and devotion."

To their report, the examiners from Poitiers added a statement. Because of the distressing condition of France, the threatened loss of Orléans, and the possible murder or capture of the Dauphin, the examiners suggested that the seventeen-year-old Jeanne d'Arc be allowed to see what she could do.

14

More Friends, More Delays, and a Sword

During the weeks of this long, drawn-out examination, Joan had made many new friends. Perhaps the best friend she made was one of the royal dukes, the charming and worldly Duke d'Alençon.

This nobleman, like Jean de Metz before him, believed in Joan's story from the very first moment he saw her.

One night d'Alençon came to dine with the Dauphin and the Dauphin's chief counselor. Joan was also present. After the stiff and formal dinner, the Duke decided to give Joan some fun. He took her into a nearby field, where he taught her to ride and use a lance as she galloped along. Joan managed it all so skillfully that the Duke was astonished.

Later, while waiting to have her name cleared by the council at Poitiers, the Duke took Joan to stay with his mother and his beautiful young wife. These two noblewomen became very fond of the farm girl from Domrémy, and she of them. When Joan left her new friends, she begged the Duke's worried young bride not to cry at her husband's departure. She, Joan, would bring him safely home from the wars.

But it was not easy to convince the tearful bride that Joan really would return her husband unharmed. How could the girl be so positive?

Poor Joan had little time for reassuring her friend. During her stay at Poitiers her examiners thought it necessary to go once more into the matter of her clothing. Joan had steadfastly refused to wear girl's clothes; to do so, she said, would be to disobey her Voices. It was also good sense for a girl leading as active a life as Joan's.

55

But before long a rumor got around that Joan was not a girl but a boy. It was said she was just pretending to be a girl. So, among her other trials, Joan had to be examined by a body of ladies-in-waiting at the Dauphin's court. They formally declared her to be a girl.

At last all the examinations were over and Joan's record was clear. She was free to depart for the besieged city of Orléans. She was sure her victory would not be an easy one, but she was anxious to begin the tasks that lay before her.

The French people who knew about Joan were also eager that she begin her mission. Something about her simple confidence and courage gave people hope. When the French heard about the farm girl from Lorraine who had such faith in herself and in the winning of the war against the invaders, they took heart. A new hope began to grow in the suffering countryside.

Before Joan started off to the wars she was

equipped in a truly royal manner befitting her new station in life. She was to ride forth with the armies in company with two personal pages, two heralds, her own private chaplain, and a groom for her own horse. A suit of armor, specially constructed of light steel plates, was made for her. Her horse, too, was given special armor. She ordered a white banner to carry in battle, and someone gave her a little axe.

Last of all Joan had to have a sword.

Joan knew exactly what sword she wanted. Her Voices had told her to send a messenger to the Church of St. Catherine in a little village not far from Tours, where she was then staying. Behind the altar, they told her, an old sword would be found. It would be lying in an unused rusty coffer that had not been opened for many years.

The messengers went, following Joan's instructions. When the coffer was found, it was pried open by the priests of the church.

Inside was a rusty and dirty sword, just as Joan had described.

After it was cleaned—and the church people said the rust came off "like magic"—it was found to have five crosses engraved on its blade. The church authorities agreed that Joan might have the sword since she had seen it in a vision.

Later it was discovered that the sword had originally belonged to an ancient Frankish king called Charles Martel.

The people of the town of Tours were greatly impressed with this newest miracle of Joan's and made her two sheaths in which to carry her sword. One was a rich velvet, one of gold cloth. Then Joan, practical as always, instructed that a strong leather sheath should also be made.

Joan did not intend to use the sword, for it was not her wish to kill anyone. But she did realize that she might need to protect herself. As a matter of fact, her Voices had already foretold that she would be wounded. She was as certain of this as she was of the fact that she had only a limited time to carry out her mission.

In spite of her eagerness to fulfill her tasks, Joan hated death and suffering and everything about war. While she waited for her campaign to begin, she dictated a letter to the English commanders in France, urging them to go back to England while there was still time. She said she had no wish to harm them. Yet she could not help doing so if they insisted on remaining, for she had sworn to rid France of the enemy.

Can you picture what a hearty laugh this letter raised in the English camp? Who can imagine experienced English soldiers taking the threat of an ignorant "cow girl" seriously?

15

Joan Brings Food to Orléans

Priests and professors had admitted that Joan was not a witch. The weak-minded Dauphin had given her permission to risk her life on his behalf, and now she was at last ready to go with the soldiers.

She had a fine white horse to ride. She had her beautiful, specially made suit of armor, so pale in color that her soldiers thought it was white. She had her own chaplain, a priest who was to accompany her on her journey, and her own page to wait on her. She had her magic sword, and the white banner, embroidered with golden lilies, or *fleurs-de-lis*, to carry as she rode.

But best of all Joan now had her two brothers. While she had been so impatiently waiting to go to the wars, Jean and Pierre, the two younger members of the d'Arc family, had come from Domrémy to keep their sister company.

Word had reached her home village that Joan, the simple farm girl with the big ideas, had actually been received by the Dauphin. After this news, her parents could no longer doubt her mission, so her father permitted the boys to join her. Perhaps he even thought it a good idea if she had some extra protection in her amazing new life.

Joan's first wish, now that she could do what the Voices told her, was to relieve the siege of Orléans, the place that was called the "key city of France."

Orléans had long been in great peril. Inside its stout stone walls the loyal French people had been holding off the English invaders for many grim weeks.

The people of Orléans were brave fighters who had kept up their spirits in spite of the

61

constant danger of attack. But there was one thing that could scare the wits out of them. This was the English soldiers' shouts, from across the river, of the terrible word "Hurrah!"

The strange un-French noise sounded to the townspeople of Orléans like an evil war cry. They trembled with fear when they heard it.

Joan probably did not know this fact about the people of Orléans, but she did know that they must be hungry. There had been no chance to bring in food for a long time.

She started at once to make plans for getting supplies to them.

With herring, grain, olive oil, beef cattle, and much-needed salt for daily food, the convoy set forth. Joan planned to march her soldiers right to Orléans by the north bank of the river Loire.

On that side of the river, Joan already knew, there was a large camp of English soldiers. To them Joan had directed a letter that her page had written at her dictation, challenging this group of English to withdraw at once, so that she could take in food supplies.

If they refused, she wrote, she would at once attack them. She felt no doubt that the enemy would be beaten. After this she could easily ferry the supplies straight across the river by the shortest route, out of range of the fortified bridge.

But when Joan got near Orléans, she discovered that someone had changed her plans. This had been done by certain commanders among the French who did not care to take orders from a "saucebox of low birth," as they called Joan.

Many French officers were envious of her friendship with the Dauphin. It seemed that they would rather let Orléans starve than obey the orders of an ignorant peasant girl.

The new plan, unlike Joan's, was to start everything from the south bank, using sailing boats to carry supplies *upstream* five miles to a certain village. From that point they hoped to enter Orléans without arousing the English.

There was one thing wrong with this new plan. It would succeed only if the wind was blowing in the right direction. The wind must blow *upstream*.

When Joan got to the river, the wind was blowing straight *downstream*. What is more, it had been blowing in the same direction for days. Because of the river's strong and tricky currents, the use of sailing boats was made impossible.

This was one of the times when Joan lost her temper. It was raining cats and dogs on the bleak riverbank. That wrong wind was blowing very hard. Joan was weary from travel and from sleeping in the open fields in the heavy armor to which she was not yet accustomed.

So it came about that she spoke her mind to the first man who approached her. It did not matter that he was a Royal Prince and the first cousin of the Dauphin!

"Was it you who gave this new command?" she cried, interrupting the pretty speeches of welcome he was making to her.

The Dauphin's cousin, though taken aback, was able to reply with dignity, "I, and others wiser than I, gave that counsel." And he added, "I think it the wiser way and the safer."

His words made Joan even more angry. "So," she cried, "you think you know more about what is right than Heaven does? I am being guided. I know what plan will work and what will not. I bring you the finest help that was ever brought to knight or city—and you ignore it!"

As they talked, Joan was holding in her hand the beautiful white banner that a court painter had made for her. Although the wind was blowing a gale, the banner in Joan's hand was drooping as though in despair. Suddenly it blew out straight in the wind.

But the banner blew out in a new direction! The wind that had been blowing for days *downstream* had suddenly changed. It was now blowing *upstream*. This meant that the sailing boats could be used after all.

The soldiers and officers looking on were convinced that the miracle-working girl from Domrémy had been able to alter the very direction of the wind. Whether it was a miracle or not, the supplies were able to reach Orléans in record time.

The first load was escorted by Joan, who passed up the river and entered the city by its eastern gate. She came at nightfall, hoping to avoid crowds. But the happy people turned out by the thousands. They came with lanterns and torches to get a better look at her tired young face under her metal hood. They pressed around her horse so that she could hardly ride, and they cheered her and called her by name.

But by now Joan was only a weary young

girl. She could hardly wait to get to bed at the home of the Treasurer of the Duke of Orléans, where she was to stay. She shared a bed with the little daughter of the household, a child of nine. Probably the descendants of this little girl boast today about the night their great-great–many times great-grandmother slept with the "Savior of France."

16

Joan's First Battles

In the next week after she got the first supplies to Orléans, Joan had a busy and exciting time.

Following her triumphant entry into the besieged city, she took only a short rest. She had too much to do to spend her time in the comfortable house of the Treasurer.

First of all she tried again to warn the English about what was going to happen to them. Going out onto the bridge between Orléans and the nearest English fort, she shouted to the enemy to go home and leave the French alone.

They shouted right back. And what they had to say was not very polite. They called her "cow girl" and warned her that if they caught her they would burn her. Strangely enough, they made no attempt to shoot her with their arrows.

Joan calmly called them "liars" and went back inside the walls of Orléans. There she waited for the rest of the army and more food supplies.

It is puzzling to wonder why the English did not attack Orléans during this time of delay. They must have seen the supplies coming in, but perhaps they did not take Joan seriously. Or perhaps they simply hoped to avoid more battles, for at Christmastime the English and the people of Orléans had declared a Christmas truce. They had exchanged musicians, and a French noble had given a fur coat to an English noble in return for a plate of figs.

Joan would have approved of the Christmas truce, not only because she was a religious girl but also because she hated killing. That is why she risked her life to go out on the bridge and shout at her enemies to go home and avoid more trouble.

During the days of waiting, Joan journeyed once more through the streets of Orléans on her white horse. She did this to allow the eager townspeople to get a good look at her. They had been threatening to break into the house of the Treasurer unless they were allowed to see the famous Maid.

Joan also used this time to make a careful study of the positions of the enemy. Although she always said it was her Voices that guided her, it is quite plain that she never left anything to chance. She laid careful plans.

Then, suddenly, there was action. Joan was resting one day after her midday meal when she leaped up, saying her Voices had told her there was danger. They had informed her where she was to go at once.

She leaped from her bed, called for her armor, and left so hastily that her frightened page had to hand down her banner from an upper window of the house. So fast did her horse set off that sparks flew from the stones of the road as he galloped.

The Voices had told Joan that one of the many English forts near Orléans had threatened to prevent the passage of more supplies into the city. In reply to this threat, the weary people of Orléans, who had been given new life by Joan's presence, had made a brave attack on the enemy fort.

Joan rushed into the battle holding her white and gold banner high in the air. The very sight of her gave the fighters new courage. The day was won without great effort and with small loss of life.

After this first battle, Joan dictated another note to the English. She asked them to leave while they still could. She shot the note across the river Loire with an arrow. The English picked it up and read it.

What they read was: "You, men of England,

71

who have no right to be in this kingdom of France, the King of Heaven commands you through me, Joan the Maid, to abandon your forts and to go back where you belong; which if you fail to do, I will make such a *ha-hai* as will be eternally remembered. I am writing to you for the third and last time. I shall not write any more."

There was a postscript that added that she would have sent the letter in a "more honorable manner" but they had a way of detaining messengers. If they would send back the other herald they had kept in their camp, she would "send back some of their people recently captured." She added grimly, "They are not all dead."

The English answered with more shouts of derision and laughter. This time they used such insulting terms that poor Joan burst into tears on hearing what they were calling her.

The next day, in another battle, Joan was wounded in the foot with an iron ball with spikes sticking out of it. This ball was called a caltrop.

Although her injury must have pained her very much, she did not stay home and coddle herself. She was busy preparing for the great attack on the two remaining English forts.

Before the next big battle, Joan had word from her Voices. They told her she must be prepared for an even more serious injury.

Joan called her chaplain, the priest who accompanied her, and asked him to stay near her as best he could during the day. She told him, "Tomorrow I shall have much to do, more than I ever had yet, and the blood will flow from my body above my breast."

The wound came at noon as Joan was climbing a scaling ladder to lead her men over a high wall. An arrow passed clean through her armor and into her body, piercing her just below her right collarbone. The arrow stood out "a hand's breadth behind."

Her chaplain, who was nearby, helped to

get her away from the thick of the fighting. When the armor was removed and the wound had been dressed with olive oil, she insisted on going back to her place in the battle.

Her reappearance shocked the English. They knew that the French believed in Joan's power to work miracles. The English, for their part, had been willing to think of her as a witch. But a witch would never have been wounded. If, then, she was no witch but could still return to fight after such a wound, she must indeed have strange and uncanny powers.

That day the fighting had been very hard, but the English were still stubbornly hanging on to their chief fort. The French commander, Dunois, decided that his troops should stop for the day.

Joan asked him to wait just a little while. She went apart into a vineyard by herself to pray and think. When she returned a half hour later, she again took her white and gold standard into her hands. Holding it aloft, she began to move through her army.

By now it was dusk. The white banner glimmered eerily in the fading light. Both English and French were watching it. The English watched with dread; the French with hope.

Both sides saw the white banner move over a last ditch to a certain place at the wall of the fort. This was the spot at which Joan wanted her men to make one last attempt.

The sight of the wounded girl with the white banner inspired the French to new heights of courage. They fairly leaped over the walls of the fort, in spite of the English guns and arrows.

At this fresh attack the English fell into a panic. The bridge by which they had planned to retreat had been set on fire by a boat covered with tar. The English commander, his leading officers, and most of his army tried to cross by this bridge. It sank under them, and every man was drowned.

At last Orléans was relieved! The English had been defeated. Now Joan could return to the house of the Treasurer, where a surgeon could treat her wound.

The happy people of Orléans paraded by torchlight. They lit bonfires and danced in the streets for joy while Joan lay wounded in bed.

17

The Maid of Orléans Fights More Battles

Orléans was not the only battle won by Joan. But it was the first, and in many ways the most important. It proved what she could do.

After that she was known as the Maid of Orléans, and by that title she is also known to this day.

While Orléans was still celebrating the victory, Joan went to visit the Dauphin. They met on horseback. Joan rode up to him with her famous white banner in her hand. She respectfully bowed "right down to the saddle" at the sight of her Prince.

But the Dauphin told her to sit erect. He was so delighted with her that an onlooker said, "It was thought that he would have liked to kiss her, so glad he was."

Although he was very pleased, he still would not do what Joan asked him to do. She wanted him to go at once and be crowned the King at Reims.

She knew France must have a real leader, a crowned head. The country would have no unity until this came to pass.

The Dauphin persuaded Joan to come back to court with him. He promised to make his plans from there.

So Joan returned with the Dauphin to the court life that she heartily disliked. She was particularly bored with the simpering elegant ladies. She could not understand why they had to invent special elaborate games to amuse themselves. *Her* trouble was quite different! She had too much to do and too little time in which to do it.

But she was willing to stay at the court, for she hoped to persuade the Dauphin that he must hurry. Whenever she saw him, she pestered him to agree to go to Reims. He kept putting her off. There were many difficulties about making the trip, he said, and life was so comfortable where he was.

As usual, he could not make up his mind.

So, finally, since the English were still undefeated in many other parts of France, Joan went back to her battles.

Many stories have come down in history from those long weeks of Joan's life as a common soldier.

There is the story of how Joan saved the Duke d'Alençon from death. Do you remember that she had promised his weeping wife to bring the Duke safely home from the wars?

One day, in the thick of battle, Joan galloped past d'Alençon and cried to him above the noise, "Change your position. That gun will kill you."

The Duke moved away at once. Soon after, a man occupying the same place was killed by the gun at which Joan had pointed.

79

This was considered a miraculous deed of Joan's, but it was probably nothing more than a proof of her coolness in time of excitement. Even in the thick of a dangerous battle Joan did not lose her powers of observation. There are things about Joan of Arc that we cannot explain easily. They do seem to indicate mysterious and special powers. But much of her success came from her sharp eyes and sound common sense.

But Joan was not as careful of herself as she was of others. On the very day she saved the Duke's life, Joan herself was struck.

She was wounded as she had been in the Battle of Orléans, while climbing a scaling ladder to get over a wall into a town. A stone fired from the mouth of an enemy cannon ripped through her white banner, crashed on her helmet, and knocked her over. She fell to the ground with a heavy thud.

But almost at once she got to her feet. She knew how much her presence meant to the soldiers. When they saw her again leading the way, they lost their fear.

She lifted her torn flag and cried, "On, friends, on! Have good heart! Within an hour we take them."

And they did.

On another day there had been a bad mix-up. Careless sentries had allowed a band of English soldiers to slip through their hands. Where had they gone? No one knew.

Everyone was very upset and worried in the French headquarters. At such a time people turned to Joan. She was quite confident that everything would be all right.

When the officers asked her what they should do, she said very calmly, "Ride boldly on. You will have good guidance."

Later, when the Duke d'Alençon asked for more advice, she added, "You will need good spurs. You will all have to ride fast."

That was all she would, or could, say at the time.

Eighty mounted scouts were sent out at once to find the fleeing English. In one part of that wooded and hilly country, the scouts had to creep through the underbrush. Suddenly they startled a sleeping stag. It jumped up and bounded away.

As luck would have it, the stag bounded right through the hidden English camp. When the English soldiers caught a glimpse of the noble animal they had so often hunted, they forgot their caution. They gave a great shout, and the noise revealed their whereabouts to the searching French.

The scouts rushed back to Joan and the Duke with the news.

Soldiers set out at once. They surprised the English and threw them into great disorder. The enemy fled, leaving everything behind.

The French followed on their heels and killed and captured almost all of them.

Although Joan was glad at the victory, she wept because so many men had died. Seeing one of her own men strike a wounded Englishman on the head, she rode up at a gallop and severely scolded her soldier.

After dismounting, she took the dying man's head in her lap. When she saw that he was beyond hope, she called for a priest to tend him in his dying moments. For Joan, though as brave as the toughest among her soldiers, never lost the tender heart for which she had been known back in the little village of Domrémy.

There are many of these stories of Joan's very human qualities. They make her seem real and endearing.

She was sometimes inclined to be a little bossy. She couldn't, for instance, ever stand to hear her soldiers swear. She tried to get them to use her own harmless expressions as substitutes for their stronger oaths. It was her wish that her men be devout and go to church regularly. Great nobles and captains were ordered about by the Maid as if they were ordinary soldiers.

Joan's kind of courage counted particularly in the sort of battles that were fought at that time. In those days there were no maps with pins stuck in them—maps made by men far away from the actual fighting. The battles in which Joan fought were hand-to-hand encounters. Everyone was in them together—officers and men. A duke and a common soldier might find themselves climbing side by side up the same wall.

That is why Joan's presence had such an effect on the French soldiers. When they saw a mere girl bravely going right along in front of them, dodging stones and arrows, they had to believe she possessed some very special powers.

Yet when Joan was wounded and when she was insulted, she sometimes cried. She was, in many ways, a perfectly normal girl in her teens. But there was this difference. She knew she had a great task to perform for her country. Nothing could ever shake her faith in her mission.

18

Joan Prepares the Way to Reims

And now once again Joan tried to get the Dauphin to go to Reims to be crowned.

She had succeeded beyond anyone's wildest dreams in carrying out the first part of her mission.

The Loire Valley was cleared of the enemy. The French had captured the great English commander, Talbot. The second in command of the English army, Sir John Fastolf, had been forced to fly for his life.

And yet in spite of all Joan had done for her Prince and for her country, the Dauphin would not grant her request. He hemmed and hawed and put off going to Reims. First one person and then another offered him advice. Sad to say, much of the advice was not unselfish.

Ambitious and bad men were still trying to use the Prince for their own private ends. And these men were quite willing to use Joan, too. They were glad to have her go on winning battles and risking her life while they sat comfortably at court near the Dauphin's ear.

Then, too, many nobles were not particularly interested in ideas of national unity. They had lived for years like petty kings in their own small domains. They were used to staying safe behind their own walls and ignoring the troubles of their neighbors. They were not yet prepared to give up their privileges.

One of the greatnesses of Joan of Arc was her vision of a France that would be one country, under one ruler. She would not give up her dream of seeing the Dauphin crowned as King. She felt that he would be a symbol of French unity. So she went on working toward this end.

There were some nobles and towns that

could be trusted. So Joan decided to pull them into line!

She started to do this by riding forth on a mission to the three cities of Auxerre, Troyes, and Châlons.

The people of these three cities were afraid that if they allowed the Dauphin to travel through on his way to Reims, they would be punished by the pro-English Burgundians. To overcome their fears, Joan used her simple country-girl charm. She tried persuasion. She even used threats.

Finally she conquered the fears of these people and got permission to pass through with her Prince.

Now there remained only the city of Reims itself to win over. When Joan got there, she found the English governor away on a visit. The townsfolk said they would welcome the Dauphin. The Dauphin, who had followed safely behind Joan, was near at hand. She went out in haste to bring him at once to the ancient city where the Kings of France were always crowned.

19

The Prince Is Crowned

Joan and the Dauphin rode together into Reims. They came in through the gate that was called the Light of God. The number of people who turned out to see the Maid was as great as—or greater than—the number of those who turned out to see their future King.

As Joan made her way through the crowds, she was happy and smiling. She was, for this brief moment, at peace. She had fought and won many battles. She had survived three wounds. She was about to see the crowning of the new King of France.

Although they arrived on a Saturday and the coronation of a king must, by tradition, be held on a Sunday, Joan refused to allow a week's delay. Times were too uncertain. So was the mind of the Dauphin. They must prepare for the great event overnight.

What a fuss and bustle went on in Reims in the next few hours! No one slept. There was far too much to do.

In Reims, busy, excited Joan had still another great surprise and joy. Her father and all her family had come from Domrémy. She was told that the grateful Dauphin was planning to give them a title of honor. The dazed and happy d'Arc family had rooms in the center of the village at the Sign of the Zebra. This inn was directly across from the Cathedral, where the coronation was to take place.

What a meeting it must have been! Joan had not seen her father since the day she had left Domrémy for Vaucouleurs. Then she had been wearing a patched red dress as she rode on a borrowed farm horse. Now she was resplendent in green tunic, shining armor, a cloak of gold and crimson. She had her own blooded horse, her own household servants, pages, a major-domo, even her own chaplain. And the soon-to-be King of France was her protector.

Although there is no record of Joan's reunion with her family, we know from something she did that the occasion made her happy. To show her love for her family and friends, she asked the Prince to relieve her village, and a neighboring one, of the payment of taxes forever.

The Prince agreed to Joan's request. There exists a paper showing all levies against these two villages canceled. Beside the notice of the cancellation, written in the Prince's own hand, are the words *Nothing, the Maid!*

By these words the Prince was explaining, to anyone who was curious, why he had left such a special order: *Nothing, because the Maid requested it.*

It was not until three hundred years later that the taxes were once more levied against these villages.

During the days in Reims, Joan slept in the house of the Archbishop. The Prince and his court were also placed there.

This Archbishop had not occupied his own home for over twenty years. The English had kept him out. So it was a great day for him, too, when Joan rode into Reims. But, later, we shall see that this Archbishop forgot what he owed to the girl who had restored him to his home.

However, on that day in Reims, there was no thought of ingratitude or injustice. The air was filled with too much joy.

The morning of the coronation dawned bright and sunny with cloudless skies. All the people were happy and full of new hope for their country. Men and women put on their very best clothes and paraded the streets while they waited for the great event to take place.

The sacred oil that was used to anoint all Kings of France on their coronation days was brought from the church in which it had long been hidden. But no one could find the King's crown. It had been hidden too well. However, another crown was found that could be used, although it was not a very fine one. Later the real crown was discovered.

Joan rode proudly through the streets to the Cathedral. She had been placed at the head of the procession beside the Prince. She also stood beside him throughout the ceremony in the church. This was an honor that not even the greatest nobleman had ever had before. In her hand Joan held her white standard embroidered with golden lilies. She had insisted on bringing this banner with her.

"It has been through so many dangers," she said, "it must share in the hour of glory."

When the King was at last crowned, the trumpets burst into loud blasts of triumph. People shouted and wept for joy. Joan knelt at the feet of the new King. She made one of her solemn speeches to the man for whom she had done so much.

"Gentle King, now is accomplished the Will of God, Who decreed that I should raise the siege of Orléans and bring you to this city of Reims to receive your solemn anointing, thereby showing that you are the true King, and that France should be yours."

Once more, as on other occasions, the Dauphin tried to lift this strange, solemn, wonder-working farm girl to her feet. But Joan was overcome. She knelt weeping on the floor while the waves of triumphant sound from trumpets and voices rose and broke around her in the nave of the great Cathedral.

20

Joan Goes On Fighting

After Reims, Joan's real troubles began.

She had accomplished wonderful things in the few months since she left the village of Domrémy. But there was still much left to be done. And, as always, Joan worried about delays because she knew that her time for accomplishing her mission was to be a short one.

She also longed to go back to the farm. Perhaps her family's visit had made her homesick. One day, as she rode out with the Archbishop of Reims and the King's cousin, she spoke of her longing for home.

"I do wish that the good God would allow me to lay down my arms and go back to Domrémy with my father and my mother.

How nice it would be to tend sheep again along with my sister and my brothers."

Joan was always hoping for an end to the war. Three weeks before the coronation she had written the Duke of Burgundy urging him to consider a peace plan. On the very day of the coronation she had written again asking him to help bring the weary war to an end.

In this instance Joan's goodness and her lack of worldly wisdom played right into the scheming Duke's hand. He sent off a message saying that he would be happy to consider a truce. He even sent envoys to the King to talk it over. He implied that he would be ready to give up the important city of Paris, which the Burgundians held along with the English. Perhaps he knew that Paris was Joan's next point of attack.

The newly crowned King was, as usual, happy to have disagreeable things postponed. He gladly agreed to the terms of the Duke of

Burgundy's truce. But a part of the terms was a fifteen-day period of waiting for final discussions.

Here wise Joan smelled a rat. She sensed that such a delay would only give the English time to send fresh troops to Paris, and she sensed also that the Duke was not sincere.

It was another matter to influence the King to her way of thinking. For one thing, evil advisers, some of them bribed by the Duke of Burgundy himself, were whispering day and night into the King's ears. They told him that peace would allow him to return in safety to a comfortable life at court. Joan urged him not to trust the Duke's plan. To do so, she said, would actually mean only further discomfort and more of the responsibilities that the King was forever trying to avoid.

Always a weakling, though, the King listened to Joan's enemies. For a long time he could not decide what to do.

Joan felt this period of delay very keenly.

She knew that all eyes were now on the newly crowned King. She felt only shame for the way he was behaving. In a letter to the good people of Reims, she tried to make the situation clear to them. A copy of this letter has survived.

"Joan the Maid," she wrote, "sends you news of herself and requests that you shall be in no doubt as to the good quarrel that she pursues for the blood royal, and I promise and guarantee that I will never abandon you while I live."

She then went on to explain that it was true that the King had gone so far as to make a fifteen-day truce with the Duke of Burgundy, in the belief that the Duke would, at the end of it, deliver the city of Paris quite peacefully and without bloodshed. But she said she herself did not believe in the truce. She still suspected treachery and was going to be ready to act if, at the end of the truce, war was resumed. She spoke of her continuing concern for the "King's honor."

Her last lines were: "I will keep the King's army together in readiness, lest at the end of the fifteen days they should not make peace."

Joan's fears that fighting was not yet over and that there was treachery afoot came to pass. When she did march on Paris, the event was a disaster. Not only did Joan's army suffer its first serious defeat, but, during the fighting, she received another wound. This time the arrow went right through her armor into her thigh.

After the Paris disaster the King ordered the army to be disbanded. He also ordered Joan to return to court.

Brokenhearted, Joan left her famous armor lying before a statue in a cathedral. She said a last farewell to her favorite duke, the Duke d'Alençon. Then, obediently, she went back to the King's court as he had commanded.

Poor Joan began to live a life that was almost one of luxurious captivity. The King would not let her return to Domrémy. Neither would he let her go on winning the rest of the country for him.

Nine slow and boring months went by. From these months of court life, some small pictures of Joan have come down to us. She disliked playing dice—a common court pastime—and did not think well of those who wasted their time in such pleasures. She was extremely generous in giving charity. She never lost her sense of humor, nor did she set herself up as a special kind of person.

The story is told of some women who came bringing their rosaries for her to touch, as though her touch were sacred. Joan burst out laughing at this request. She said, "Touch them yourselves. They will benefit from your touch quite as much as from mine."

After some time had passed, the King asked Joan to lead an army once more. The town of St. Pierre-le-Moûtier had to be taken.

Here again Joan displayed her power to

lead men to superhuman deeds by her own example.

When the battle seemed lost, one of the French captains saw Joan fighting almost alone. Jumping on a horse (though his leg was badly injured), the captain galloped up to her.

Above the noise he shouted angrily, "What in Heaven's name are you doing here alone?"

"Alone?" Joan cried back. "I am not alone. I am with a company of fifty thousand."

After this flight of bravado, however, she added, practical as ever, "Go tell the men to gather faggots and sticks. We are going to bridge the moat."

Raising her voice and her banner, Joan called to her fleeing men, "Come back! Come back! We will yet win the day."

They could never resist the Maid's demands. Once again her magic cast its old spell. The men returned. They won the battle.

After this episode, in spite of her success, the shadows began to darken around Joan.

She could not persuade the King of the treachery of the Burgundians. He would not listen to her warnings or to her advice, but neither would he let her go. He said he still needed her.

So Joan remained at court with nothing at all to do that she thought important. Even her Voices now fell silent. She was worried about the rest of her mission. Nothing in the life she was living interested her deeply. The King tried to please her with childish gifts. He had special rich cloaks designed for her to wear. Joan took a normal interest in the richness and brightness of these court garments, but she never remained interested in them for more than a few moments.

As a final reward for Joan's services, the King gave the d'Arcs from Domrémy a coat of arms. How strange it must have been for the simple farming family to find themselves entitled to an emblem of nobility! This was a blue shield on which were two golden lilies;

between the lilies, a sword supported a crown. The design was a symbol of what Joan had done for France.

But not even the ennobling of her family kept Joan from her worry and her longing to finish the task she felt had been assigned to her.

After the long dull winter, spring came at last. The armies were again to be sent into the field.

Joan demanded to go with them, and the King finally gave his consent. Although he provided her with troops and money, he did not accompany her himself. Nor, this time, did she have her faithful Duke d'Alençon.

In the campaign on which Joan was embarked, her men were rough soldiers-of-fortune from all parts of Europe. They were mercenaries, those rough professional men who were paid to fight the wars of others.

Though Joan was glad to be free of the dull life at court, her heart was not light. She had, however, again heard from her Voices. But what they said to her was ominous. She reported this message: "They warned me that I should be captured before Midsummer Day."

21

Joan Is Captured

Joan marched her troops to the town of Compiègne, another key spot in France. At that time, Compiègne was in danger of falling into the hands of the Burgundians, who were still hoping that their ally, England, would win this long, long war.

Joan had laid sound plans for the relief of Compiègne. She knew just where she wanted her archers and crossbowmen placed during the battle. She had planned to put boats on the river outside the city's walls. These boats would carry more men with bows and arrows. She, on horseback, would lead the main attack along a certain causeway.

It was about five o'clock in the morning when Joan and her troop left their hidden camp. As usual, Joan was riding ahead of her men. She carried a banner, though it was not her famous standard, painted with lilies. Over her suit of armor she was wearing a scarlet coat embroidered in gold.

As she rode with her men toward Compiègne, the commander of the main Burgundian forces was just returning to his own camp. He had been visiting some of his outposts. By chance he looked down from a hilltop and saw Joan and her troop on the road below.

At once he guessed what was up. Gathering the few troops he had at hand, the commander sent messengers at top speed for reinforcements from the outposts.

Then, suddenly and without warning, the Burgundian soldiers fell upon Joan.

She and her small band of followers fought like demons. But as they struggled, enemy reinforcements began to arrive in large numbers. The fresh troops came so fast that Joan had no chance to carry out any of her carefully laid plans. Instead, she found herself fighting for her life.

Ordering her men to retreat along the road they had come, Joan lingered behind. It was her hope to protect them as they retreated.

In this hour of her greatest peril, Joan showed her usual daring. Three times she charged into the enemy. Each time the fury of her attack scattered them and drove them back. Yet she must have known that only a miracle could save her and her followers, for they were greatly outnumbered.

Joan was fighting not far from the drawbridge that led into the city of Compiègne. Perhaps the thought occurred to her that it might provide the means of escape. But the way was cut off when the commanding officer at Compiègne ordered the drawbridge to be raised.

This action was not taken in order to hurt Joan. The commander must have wanted with all his heart to save her. But he saw that if he kept the gate open for Joan, nothing would prevent the enemy's entering in large numbers. He had no choice but to close it.

What Joan felt when the drawbridge was clanking shut we shall never know. But we do know she did not stop fighting. Her enemies were closing in around her. On every side she saw their fierce, sweating faces. She saw their bloody swords raised against her. Cruel hands were reaching out to seize her. A great fist closed on the bridle of her horse. Clutching fingers snatched at her scarlet cloak and tore it from her body. She still had her suit of armor. It might yet protect her from a fatal wound. And she still had her sword, too. More and more wildly she used it to thrust about her.

Then a burly archer leaped to the back of her horse. He seized her arms and held them pinioned behind her. Holding her thus, he pulled her from the horse onto the ground.

Weighed down by her heavy armor, with her hands tied, she was at last helpless.

There she lay in the mud at the enemy's feet, and not a friendly hand could lift a sword to help her. All her men had been killed or captured. Even her own brothers were prisoners of the Burgundians.

Her triumphant captors took away Joan's sword. She had already lost her banner. Gone was the bright red cloak with which she had fared forth so bravely at dawn that morning. The Burgundians lifted her roughly out of the mud. When she was on her feet, they marched her off to the enemy camp.

What shouts went up when this battered, muddy, bruised young girl was led into the Burgundian camp! And how men ran to get a look at the Witch from Lorraine!

But the archer who had captured her did not delay in taking Joan straight to his commanding officer. He was in a hurry to establish his claim to the capture of the Maid of

Orléans. He was well aware that there had never been a greater prize of war. He was sure that he would, in time, receive a large reward.

And he did. Later he was given two hundred gold francs a year for life.

The archer's commanding officer was the Duke of Luxembourg. It was the Duke's sharp eyes that had seen Joan and her companions on the road that fatal morning.

With the Duke of Luxembourg when Joan was brought into his presence was the most famous man among the enemy, the Duke of Burgundy himself. The Duke of Burgundy had not arrived in time for the fighting, but he had arrived in time to witness Joan brought in as a captive.

The two dukes were overjoyed at their good luck, but they could hardly believe their eyes.

So *this* was the girl who had become a legend in two great kingdoms! Could this really be the wonder-working French witch who stood before them? Here was only a muddy, disheveled girl in dirty and bloody armor.

Had she really been able to outwit generals, order dukes about, win the loyalty of the roughest soldiers, and get a prince crowned king? It was hardly believable.

Yet the Duke of Burgundy knew that it was true. He hastily put pen to paper and wrote a boastful letter about what had happened. He was able to report, he said, that in the latest engagement the Burgundian forces had lost no men by either killing or imprisonment. Yet the enemy had suffered grievous losses. Most wonderful of all, Joan the Maid had been taken prisoner! Now perhaps the French people would see how foolish they had been to believe the girl had any special powers.

22

Joan Is a Prisoner

Although when Joan was taken prisoner her brothers had also been captured, the boys were soon ransomed and allowed to return to their comrades.

One brother settled down to live in Orléans, the city his sister's courage had saved for France. The other became a captain in the army. In time he succeeded to the post at Vaucouleurs that had been occupied at the beginning of Joan's marvelous career by the rough, tough commander Robert de Baudricourt. Do you remember how de Baudricourt had laughed at Joan before his faith in her became so great that he sent her to the Dauphin?

Once more, people were laughing at poor

Joan of Arc. But you may be sure they did not treat her carelessly; she was still much too valuable a prize. Indeed, the Duke of Luxembourg went so far as to put her up in his own house. Here his wife and an aunt were assigned to care for the Maid.

The Duke's elegant old aunt was very much shocked when Joan refused to take off her boy's clothes. Joan said her Voices told her long ago to wear these garments and to continue to do so until the Voices gave her permission to change them.

The ladies of the Duke's household became quite fond of the sad, crestfallen Maid of Orléans. Joan returned their kindness with gratitude. But her heart was far away.

She was given no news of what was happening to the rest of France. She worried particularly about the fate of the city of Compiègne, which had been her own downfall. She had heard a terrible rumor that the enemy planned to massacre everyone

113

there over seven years of age.

No one could, or would, relieve Joan's mind. Her guiding Voices had again fallen silent. She had nothing to reassure or comfort her.

Day and night Joan lived in the dread that she herself would fall into English hands. The Burgundians were bad enough. They were the enemy, but they were at least French.

Her fear of being handed over to the English, and perhaps also her wish to get back to the people who needed her, led Joan to a desperate deed.

She was imprisoned in a tower room of the Duke's castle. The window of this tower was sixty feet from the ground. Joan made up her mind to jump from it. She said afterward that her Voices forbade her, but she went against their advice.

No one believes that Joan meant to kill herself by this desperate deed. She wanted only to escape. We do not know whether she jumped, or whether someone had smuggled her a rope that broke with her weight. In any case she jumped, or fell, sixty feet to the ground.

She was found lying beneath the tower, quite unconscious. The people who found her thought at first that she was dead. But when they carried her back to the tower, they found her miraculously still alive. Not one bone had been broken. She was only severely bruised and shaken.

For two days and nights Joan lay without speaking or eating. Then strength seemed to flow back into her body. She said that her Voices had at last promised her that Compiègne would be saved.

This event finally came to pass. Although the King sent no help to the stricken town, its brave citizens and the commander who had had to close the bridge fought on bravely. At last the people of Compiègne forced the enemy to retreat. Later it was realized that this retreat was one of the turning points in the long English-French struggle. Wise Joan had been among the first to realize the importance of this city.

Joan, in her prison room, did not know any of the details about Compiègne. But she had been comforted by the promises made by her Voices. She bore the next phase of her imprisonment as bravely as she could.

This second period of Joan's prison life was one of real torture for a girl who had lived outdoors in the sun, light, and air all her eighteen years. For now, because she had jumped from a window, Joan was put into a room that had no opening to the air or sky.

Day and night became the same. There was only darkness, inaction, silence.

Silence from everyone! No word came about a possible ransom. There were no messages from friends. There was no sign that she was remembered by the King, who owed her so much, the Duke d'Alençon, who had taught her to ride, or any of the other comrades of her days of glory. Even her family in Domrémy, and her ransomed brothers, seemed to have forgotten her.

Looking back from this point in history, it is hard to understand the ingratitude of the King and the Duke d'Alençon, whose life Joan had saved. Perhaps the Duke did suffer later from painful regrets. In any event, after Joan was gone, his life took a turn for the worse. With the passing of the years, the Duke d'Alençon went slowly to pieces. In the end he was to die a drunkard and insane.

So far as we know, only one plot was hatched to rescue the girl who had done so much for her countrymen. This plot was worked out by those rough hired men-of-arms with whom she had most recently served. Unhappily, however, their amateurish scheme was discovered.

For a while Joan had hoped that she might

get away through an exchange of prisoners on a high level. But who among the English or the Burgundians was as valuable as the Maid?

As for ransoming her, how could the poor French people raise enough money? Consider the city of Orléans. Joan had saved it, and everyone there was grateful to her. But the city of Orléans had not even been able to raise enough money to ransom its own Duke. The unhappy Duke of Orléans had been a prisoner in England for fifteen years—ever since the great battle of Agincourt, fought when Joan was still a baby. And it was certainly plain that Joan of Arc was worth a great deal more than any mere duke.

In the end Joan's worst fear came to pass. The English bought her from their allies, the Burgundians. Ten thousand gold francs were to be handed over to the Duke of Luxembourg in return for Joan, the Maid of France.

23

Dark Forces Gather

Far away from the guarded room in which a defeated young girl paced the floor in sadness and despair, great events were slowly taking shape. Around the person of Joan the Maid dark forces were gathering.

Joan was not abandoned, though she must have felt that she was. She had many friends, but they could not make their strength felt. Soldiers and peasants and simple priests, and the ordinary citizens of the town through which Joan had passed with her armies—all of them wished her well. But how were they to join together and pit themselves against such powerful figures as dukes and archbishops? So all Joan knew was that suddenly she seemed to have no friends left; only enemies.

Even the Archbishop of Reims—the man who had regained his home and cathedral because of Joan's services—even he made strong charges against her. He said she would not listen to anyone's advice.

Although this Archbishop did not take an active part in Joan's persecution, another Bishop, Pierre Cauchon, the Bishop of Beauvais, was quite willing to speak up.

The name Pierre Cauchon is one to remember. This Bishop had always been on the Burgundian side. On one occasion when Joan came through with the King's armies, he had been forced to fly from his district. Then, by fatal chance, Joan was captured in his diocese. Probably Cauchon felt revengeful. He also, apparently, was sincerely convinced that Joan was in the power of the Devil. He could not understand her successes in any other way.

Pierre Cauchon, the Bishop of Beauvais, used all the means at his command to get Joan placed in the hands of the English for her trial. Perhaps he felt that the English would not feel as sentimental about her as other Frenchmen—even Burgundians—might.

Certainly the English were anxious to get Joan out of the way. They believed that if she were gone, the weakling King would never be able to hold out against them. They were certain, too, that this peasant sorceress, this witch, had caused all their recent troubles and threatened their hold in France.

What is more, the English leaders told themselves that they would be doing a very fine thing if they got rid of this strange girl. They had to respect Joan for her amazing deeds in the field of war, but they were sure the power to do the deeds came from the Devil.

The leading English duke, the Duke of Bedford, was still hoping to get his nephew, a little English prince, crowned King of France in spite of what had happened at Reims. The

Duke of Bedford expressed the general English opinion of Joan. He called her "that limb of the Fiend."

Certainly no eighteen-year-old girl ever had so many learned and powerful men interested in her fate. Although she herself could not read or write, the most brilliant professors at the University of Paris did nothing but talk about her. And as they talked, they tried to explain her power.

These men of intellect had at first pooh-poohed the legendary gifts of an illiterate farm girl. Later they had come to believe that Joan *had* worked miracles. If so—they agreed with the English—surely only the Devil himself could be responsible! It was not possible for them to believe that wisdom might be present in a girl who had never received any education.

The group of men in Paris who were studying Joan's case—at a pleasant distance from her lonely prison—ignored the verdict handed down months before by the University of Poitiers.

You remember how the Dauphin commanded these first professors and priests to examine Joan thoroughly before he gave permission for her to start for Orléans? And how these men had reported that they found nothing in the girl from Domrémy but "honesty, simplicity, humility, maidenhood, and devotion"?

How far away—as far as another world—these hours in Poitiers must have seemed to Joan, if, indeed, she thought of them at all. At that first examination, Joan had been a confident and eager girl. She had not yet known failure. She believed completely in the direction of her Voices. She had even been a little cheeky with her examiners, so buoyant was she in her youth and health.

Now she felt quite helpless. No one told her anything. No one talked with her. She was moved about like a pawn in some mysterious chess game. She did not even know who was moving her around on the imaginary board.

After the English, urged on by Pierre Cauchon, offered the ten thousand gold francs for Joan, they had to collect the ransom money. This was apt to take some time because they had to get the money out of the people. And after almost a hundred years of war, people everywhere were poor.

While waiting for the money, the Duke of Luxembourg and his advisers decided to move Joan farther north. They felt there would be less chance of her escape or rescue on the northern seacoast.

So Joan found herself living in a French castle on the English Channel. This was not an unpleasant place. She relaxed a little here. Her beloved Voices returned to her again and spoke with her. She was allowed a room with a window and she could look down on a little fishing village and a pretty harbor.

Joan may or may not have known that this was the very same harbor from which William the Conqueror set sail from France in 1066 to invade England. If she did know it, did she say to herself that, in a way, all her troubles had begun with this famous soldier? For if William the Conqueror had not conquered England, his descendants would not have been in France now, waging the Hundred Years' War.

Whether she thought at all about William the Conqueror, we can only imagine. She probably did think, however, of her dear Duke d'Alençon. He, too, had been a prisoner in this very same castle for five long years. The knowledge that he had been ransomed eventually from this same place may have given Joan heart.

While she was imprisoned at the castle, Joan was allowed to see a few people. Friendly priests were permitted to visit her. And a group of ladies from a nearby town came down the river, some by barges, to pay her a formal call. Curiosity had probably got the better of them. They could not resist going to have a look at this amazing member of their own sex.

As soon as the ransom money had been—with some difficulty—collected, English soldiers came for Joan. From the pleasant castle on the seacoast they ferried her across the river Somme when the tide was full. On the far bank a horse was waiting to carry Joan by slow and tedious stages to the city of Rouen.

Paris had hoped to enjoy the pleasure of trying the "unholy" Maid in their city. But they had to accept disappointment. The town of Rouen was allotted the privilege of this great spectacle.

Rouen, though in France, was still an English city. Because it was the English capital of the province of Normandy, it was chosen as the scene of Joan's trial.

As soon as she arrived in Rouen, Joan was thrown into a dark underground cell. Five men of the lowest type guarded her day and night. These jailers tied her hands together and chained her feet. Still, they feared that at night, under cover of darkness, she might perform some "miracle" and escape. So they attached still another chain around her waist and fastened it to a beam above her.

As a further precaution, an iron cage was made to put her in, should any emergency arise. Joan was never placed in this cage, but it is likely that her tormentors took occasion to describe it to her.

Here in her Rouen prison cell, Joan did not lack for visitors. They came by the dozens, all kinds and all degrees of people. There were English earls. There were church dignitaries. There were the base companions of her low guards. There was even a duchess who sent her tailor to make Joan a dress. But Joan still refused to give up her boy's clothes. She said she had had no word from her Voices about doing so.

Once, her former jailer, Jean de Luxembourg, paid her a visit. He brought with him two famous English noblemen, the Earls of Stafford and Warwick, and his own brother, an eminent French bishop.

At this meeting the Duke of Luxembourg tried to get Joan to promise never to take up arms again. He said if she would promise, he would arrange to have her ransomed.

Joan did not believe him—and it does not seem likely that he had the authority he claimed.

"What do you mean by such an offer?" she cried. "You know you haven't the power to ransom me. I belong now to the English. Have you come just to make fun of me?"

Luxembourg insisted that he had not come to laugh at her. But Joan knew the offer was a hollow one. Her old fire flared up for a moment. She said she knew quite well why the English wanted to see her dead. They thought that when she was safely out of this world, they could have all of France.

"But," she cried, "even if they were a hundred thousand more than they are now, they should not have the kingdom."

The Earl of Stafford, who was quick-tempered, drew his sword at this bold reply from a girl chained to a piece of wood. He might have killed her on the spot, but the Earl of Warwick intervened. He did not want Joan to escape the horrors of her trial by a quick death with a sword.

Continually, people tried to get from Joan a promise that she would not attempt to escape. But poor Joan was unable to tell an untruth. She always replied patiently that she could make no such promise. Because, she said, if she were to give her word and then were to escape, she would have been telling a lie.

There was, alas, little likelihood of any escape for the Maid of France!

24

The End Draws Near

Three days after her nineteenth birthday, on the ninth of January in the year 1431, Joan was placed on trial for her life.

The trial was a complicated affair. There were so many fingers in Joan's pie by this time that it was bound to drag on a long time. It actually went on for over four months.

Four months of almost daily questions! Can you imagine the strain of it?

It wasn't going to be easy to prove Joan a witch and guilty of misdeeds. It would have been far easier to have "sewn her in a sack and thrown her into a river," as someone had suggested. But she had had too spectacular a career for this kind of murder. She was a subject of interest, debate, worry, and concern to

kings, princes, dukes, generals, and archbishops. So her assassins chose to prolong her
torture in the name of "justice."

It is necessary to explain something here
about the nature of Joan's trial.

In the days when Joan lived, the Church
and the State were not yet separated as they
are in the world today. In the Middle Ages, a
person could be tried for some religious reason and actually be hanged or burned if the
judges found him guilty of being what was
called a heretic.

A heretic was anyone who did not follow
the principal beliefs of the church to which he
belonged. To try cases of heresy, there were
special courts called the Inquisition. It was in
such a court that poor Joan was accused of
being a heretic.

There was another point to the case against
Joan. She had shown that she possessed special powers of courage and the ability to
inspire men to perform superhuman deeds in

time of danger. It was well known, too, that she could sometimes foretell future events. All this led people to believe that either she was a saint, or her unusual powers were given her by the Devil.

Now not everybody who knew Joan thought her one of the Devil's handmaidens, by any means. The people who had fought beside her were quite unwilling to believe that she was evil. But, unhappily, none of the people who believed in her goodness were present at her trial.

One of the most shameful things about the trial of Joan of Arc is the fact that she was allowed no lawyer to help her defend herself. Also, she was permitted to use no witnesses on her own behalf. Furthermore, although Joan repeatedly asked that she be sent to the Pope, or failing that, to the Church Council at Basle, for a just trial, her requests were always denied. Basle and the Pope were "too far away," she was always told. Pierre

Cauchon—the Bishop of Beauvais and the chief of the trial's two judges—was certainly not on Joan's side. Any other members of the court who might have favored the Maid had been frightened into silence by either Cauchon or the English. If any of her powerful friends tried to get help to her, we know nothing about it. She had no one but herself in these black hours.

Because the trial was, in its nature, a religious trial, Joan had to answer some very difficult questions. One of the questions put to her was, "Do you think you are in a state of grace?" This was a way of asking her if she thought she was a good Christian.

This question seems to have been a trap. If Joan said "No," she would be confessing to the guilt of which they were accusing her. If she said "Yes," she would be proving what they were always saying about her, that she was very proud and "too sure of herself."

Nothing gives a clearer picture of the kind

of girl Joan of Arc was than her remarkable answer to this tricky question. Her reply was, "If I am not in a state of grace, may God bring me there; if I am, may He keep me there."

This must have taken the wind out of her accusers' sails for a few moments!

How did Joan find the courage to answer so boldly and wisely during her trial? She said she did just as her Voices told her. She managed even at times to be gay. Once, when about twenty people were shouting to her and at one another at the same time, Joan burst out laughing. "Don't all talk at once, good fathers," she cried. Instead of admiring her gallant spirit, her judges found this only another example of impudence.

They were also more shocked than amused, on another occasion, by Joan's remark to the clerk who had made a mistake in taking down some of her testimony. "If you make another mistake like that," she said, "I'll pull your ears."

Joan kept up her spirits very well. She made her protests as best she could. Once she cried out to the Bishop of Beauvais, her chief examiner, "Oh, you write the things which are against me, but not the things which are in my favor."

And again she uttered words that must have sent a cold chill down the spine of that same Pierre Cauchon.

Joan said to this stern, haughty man, "You say you are my judge; I do not know if you are or not. But be very careful not to judge me wrongly, for you would be putting yourself in grave danger. I am warning you of it now, so that if Our Lord punishes you for it, I shall have done my duty in telling you."

As the trial wore on, certain points of attack on Joan became apparent. One of these points was the matter of Joan's mysterious Voices. Her persecutors wanted Joan to admit that she had lied about them. She said she could not do so. She insisted that she had been guided to do what she had done from the day she left Domrémy. She could not retract or deny this even if it meant losing her life.

The other point of attack—and how unimportant it seems to us today—was the matter of her boy's clothes. This sensible outfit for a girl to wear who was riding every day, climbing walls, fighting, and living on equal terms with men became a special point of attack by her judges. When she refused to give up these garments (and living in prison as she was, this was surely also wise on Joan's part), her refusal was held against her. It was considered one more example of her "astonishing and monstrous brazenness."

Twice during these painful hours, days, and weeks of intense grilling, Joan fell ill. After her second illness, her captors did a dreadful thing to her. They took her into a torture chamber and showed her the thumbscrews and other terrible devices of punishment.

They hoped that Joan, weak and sick, would give way at the sight of the torture chamber and confess that she had done wrong.

When she saw the torturers and all their terrible instruments, Joan did cry aloud in fear. She shrank back against the wall and covered her face with her hands. But she would not admit that she had told lies about her Voices. She was so honest that she did say to her guards that if they tortured her she might, from pain, give in and say she had lied. But she added that the moment they released her she would say that her statements were worthless because force had been used to wring false words from her.

This was one of Joan's most terrible days as a prisoner. Did she remember that it was the anniversary of the bright day in May when she had ridden in triumph through the grateful and rejoicing city of Orléans?

At last, after four months, the trial came to an

end. There were many pages of damning testimony. Joan was formally accused by Pierre Cauchon, the Bishop of Beauvais, of telling lies. His words were: "fictitious, pernicious, and misleading lies, proceeding from evil or diabolical spirits."

This judgment having been made, there remained nothing now but to burn as a heretic Joan, the Maid of France.

25

Joan's Collapse

A few days later a public meeting was held to read the charges against Joan and to attempt to make her admit her guilt. In a cemetery near her prison two platforms had been built. One platform was to hold such dignitaries as the Bishop of Beauvais, the English commander, and other ranking notables.

The second platform was for Joan, the prisoner, and for the priests who would attend her in her last hour. In front of the two platforms an upright stake had been driven into the ground. Nearby was a pile of dry wood and other fuel for a bonfire.

As Joan was led from prison to her platform, she looked out onto a sea of vulgar and curious faces. In those days the burning of a witch was a pleasurable holiday. And Joan was considered a witch.

When they got her to her platform, a preacher rose to make a final sermon. He started off by denouncing Joan's absent protector, King Charles VII, whose crown she had won. This preacher called the former Dauphin a heretic. After all, had he not engaged the services of Joan, now proved to have been guided by the Devil?

Even in this hour of her extremity, Joan had the courage to speak out in defense of the craven King who had not so much as lifted a finger to assist her. "He is the noblest Christian alive," she cried.

"Silence her!" shouted the preacher.

When the sermon was finished, Bishop Cauchon rose. He began to read the documents of Joan's trial. He was a little over halfway through when he paused to give some of his words special emphasis.

These words were the most solemn and

dreadful words that a religious girl of the fifteenth century could hear about herself.
Bishop Cauchon announced that Joan was
now "abandoned." She was, he said, cast out
of her Church forever. She was an unregener-
ate heretic, a "limb of Satan severed from the
Church."

This statement of the Bishop's meant, for
Joan, a punishment more terrible than burning. It meant that throughout eternity she
would have no hope of salvation.

At these terrible words Joan broke down.
She began to weep and to cry out wildly. She
said over and over again that she had been
wrong, that she would do anything and everything her judges directed. She would even
give up belief in her Voices. At last she had
lost faith in her own knowledge. She was convinced that her judges must be right after all.

Wild excitement followed Joan's surprising
collapse. It was almost as though the judges
had expected—certainly hoped—that she

would break down. They had a paper ready for signing. Someone thrust a pen into her hand, and with it Joan made her mark.

In her agony, in the shouting and the tumult, it is unlikely that she heard the words of Cauchon. These fateful words still condemned her to prison for as long as she lived. Her sins were so great, stated the Bishop of Beauvais, that to the end of her days, Joan must "live on the bread of pain and the water of sorrow." Only thus, he said, could she hope for eventual forgiveness in another life.

26

The Burning

So Joan went back to her prison cell.

She was too broken in spirit to resist anything now. In complete apathy she accepted the women's clothes that were brought to her. Without complaint, almost as though she did not notice what they were doing to her, she let them tie her hands behind her. She said nothing when they bound her feet together. The same guards were outside her door.

Nothing had changed outside, only inside. Inside her own mind there was only confusion, for she had denied the truth of her guidance and the rightness of the things she had done to try to unify France.

Now began a torture even more terrible than the agony of thumbscrews or the rack.

This torture was the torture of self-accusation. What had she done? Joan asked herself. Why had she signed that paper? She *had* heard the Voices. She *had* been guided. She had done no wrongs that she could think of. She had even tried to warn the English to go home before they were killed.

Joan looked back on the few crowded years in which she had been Jeanne d'Arc, the Savior of France. She thought of the priests who had been her friends and had found her a good and pious girl. She thought of the professors who once before had examined her and found no wrong in her. She thought of the noblemen who had been willing to risk their fortunes with her. She remembered the soldiers who had been willing to die because they believed in her enough to follow her over the moats and the high stone walls of the enemy. Was all this the work of a wicked girl, a girl who had sold her soul to the Devil?

For three days and three nights Joan fought

her last and most terrible battle, a battle with her own conscience. She fought it alone, with no help from anyone.

On the third day, when priests came to call on Joan in her cell, they hardly knew her. Her face was swollen almost beyond recognition by her weeping. She was again wearing her boy's clothes.

When the visitors appeared at her prison door, Joan told them she had changed her mind about the paper she had signed. It was not true. She had recanted only because she was afraid, and because she thought perhaps her judges had been right. Now she knew better. She wanted to take back her confession. It was not true.

The priests asked her solemnly, "Do you know what this means?"

"Yes," she said. "I know. It means they will burn me."

After that, there was little time left for Joan to think or to pray.

It was a Sunday morning when she announced her change of heart. Early on Tuesday they came to tell her that this was the day of her death.

Joan was just a few days past nineteen. She was young and full of life. When she heard these final terrible words, she shrank back and sobbed. But she would not change her position.

They took her in an open cart to the old marketplace of Rouen. Everyone turned out to see the young witch drawn through the streets to her death. She was wearing a long gown, as was the custom. On her head she wore a mocking paper cap shaped like a bishop's miter. On it were painted two black demons, and between the demons four words. The four words were "Heretic. Relapsed. Apostate. Idolator." To a girl of deep faith, nothing more frightful could have been said of her.

Before soldiers set fire to Joan, another long sermon was delivered.

Then Joan was given a brief chance to speak. She uttered only a few low words. She begged forgiveness of all her friends, of her soldiers, and of her supporters, for any wrong or harm she might have done them. She asked for all their prayers. She said she forgave any evil they had done to her.

When her low young voice died on the silent air—for how carefully everyone was listening!—the Magistrate shouted the fatal command. "Away with her!"

They hustled Joan from her wagon and tied her to the stake that had been pounded in the earth.

As they were binding her, Joan turned to the company around her and asked piteously for a cross. A common English soldier, whose name no one knows, made an enduring place for himself in history with a simple act of kindness. He picked up a stick, broke it in two, tied the pieces together in the rough form of a cross, and handed it to the doomed girl.

Farther off in the crowd some other good human being went into a neighboring church and brought out a silver cross on which Joan could look from a distance.

She kept her eyes on this cross as, with the gift of her enemy clasped in her hands, she died in the mounting flames.

27

Aftermath

Joan of Arc did not die in vain.

Almost from the moment of her terrible death, the hour of France's liberation from the English began to dawn. The loss of the city of Compiègne, where Joan was captured, proved a setback from which the enemy did not recover. New resistance movements broke out among the French everywhere. Peasants who had been armed by the English turned against their masters. The English soldiers themselves began to desert their own army in larger and larger numbers.

Conditions grew really black for the enemy when King Charles VII and his old enemy the Duke of Burgundy met and signed a truce. This time the Duke really meant it when he put his name to the paper. He had severed his connections with the English. He swore his allegiance to the former Dauphin and gave up fighting forever.

Finally there was fought the last great battle between the English and the French, enemies for a hundred years. This was the battle of Castillon. In this battle died Talbot, the English general whom Joan captured at Orléans. He had been ransomed afterward by his countrymen because he was so valuable as a leader.

The death of Talbot and the loss of Castillon were English disasters. After this, town after town fell to the French. Finally the English had only one town left. This was the town of Calais on the English Channel.

Then the English gave up. Peace was declared. France was at last united under one ruler. Joan's wish, her dream, had come true.

Twenty-five years after Joan's ashes had been scattered to the winds, her family presented a petition to the Pope at Rome. It was her mother and two brothers who presented this document. Joan's father had died shortly after his daughter's trial as a heretic. People said his end had come as the result of the shame of Joan's death, and of a broken heart.

Joan's family presented their petition to the Pope because he was the head of the Church. They asked the Pope to have Joan's case retried. Although Joan's plea to see the Pope had been many times refused at the time of her trial, her family's request was now granted.

Many witnesses who had known the Maid from childhood on were allowed to give evidence about her. One hundred and twenty-five witnesses appeared at the examination. These people were of all kinds and of all classes. They were priests, simple citizens, farmers, soldiers, former neighbors, lords, dukes, and ladies.

The evidence of the one hundred and twenty-five witnesses was so overwhelming that it could not be denied. Joan's innocence was re-established. Beyond a doubt, said these people who had known her best, Joan had done only good. She had given her life to help unite her war-torn country.

From that day on, Joan of Arc has been the national heroine of France. No one in the country's history has ever occupied so warm a spot in the hearts of the French people as does the valiant Maid. The very place of her origin, the little village of Domrémy in the valley of the Meuse, bears her name. On maps of France it is written *Domrémy-la-Pucelle*. This means Domrémy of the Maid, or the Maid's birthplace.

And in the twentieth century, in the year 1920, Pope Benedict XV declared that henceforth the Maid of Orléans was to be called a saint, Saint Joan of Arc.